Homeland Security and
Counter terrorism Careers

Special Agent

and Careers in the FBI

Air Marshal
and Careers in Transportation Security
ISBN: 0-7660-2647-7

Border Patrol Agent
and Careers in Border Protection
ISBN: 0-7660-2646-9

Operations Officer
and Careers in the CIA
ISBN: 0-7660-2649-3

Search and Rescue Specialist
and Careers in FEMA
ISBN: 0-7660-2650-7

Secret Service Agent
and Careers in Federal Protection
ISBN: 0-7660-2651-5

Special Agent
and Careers in the FBI
ISBN: 0-7660-2648-5

Homeland Security and
Counter**terrorism** Careers

Special Agent

and Careers in the FBI

by Ann Graham Gaines

Enslow Publishers, Inc.
40 Industrial Road
Box 398
Berkeley Heights, NJ 07922
USA

http://www.enslow.com

5/10/07

Copyright © 2006 by Enslow Publishers, Inc.

All rights reserved.

No part of this book may be reproduced by any means without the written permission of the publisher.

Library of Congress Cataloging-in-Publication Data

Gaines, Ann.
  Special agent and careers in the FBI / Ann Graham Gaines.
    p. cm. — (Homeland security and counterterrorism careers)
  Includes bibliographical references and index.
  ISBN: 0-7660-2648-5 (alk. paper)
  1. United States. Federal Bureau of Investigation—Vocational
guidance—Juvenile literature. 2. United States Federal Bureau of
Investigation—Officials and employees—Juvenile literature. I. Title.
  HV8144.F43G35 2006
  363.25023'73—dc22
                                    2006025261

Printed in the United States of America

10 9 8 7 6 5 4 3 2 1

To Our Readers:
We have done our best to make sure all Internet Addresses in this book were active and appropriate when we went to press. However, the author and the publisher have no control over and assume no liability for the material available on those Internet sites or on other Web sites they may link to. Any comments or suggestions can be sent by e-mail to comments@enslow.com or to the address on the back cover.

Photo Credits: Associated Press, AP, pp. 3, 77, 85, 102; Corbis/Anna Clopet, pp. 65, 66, 68–69, 82, 87; Corbis/Michael Mulvey, Dallas Morning News, p. 73; Corbis/ Richard T. Nowitz, p. 16; Corbis/Reuters, p. 71; Corbis/Royalty-Free, pp. 121, 123, 125, 127; Getty Images, pp. 5, 6, 7, 8, 12, 25, 26, 31, 35, 42, 45, 60–61, 75, 95, 96, 103, 106; Getty Images/AFP, pp. 38, 40, 51; Getty Images/AFP/Stephen Jaffe, p. 78; Getty Images/AFP/Pierre Verdy, p. 104; Getty Images/AFP/Rhona Wise, p. 49; Getty Images/Time Life Pictures, p. 19; Library of Congress, pp. 5, 11, 22, 23, 28, 126, 128; Courtesy of National Science Foundation, photo by Chris Danals, pp. 5, 43, 53, 120, 122, 124; U.S. Customs & Border Protection/ James Tourtellotte, pp. 5, 83, 90–91, 111, 113, 115, 117, 119; U.S. Department of Defense, pp. 110, 112, 114, 116, 118.

Cover Photos: Associated Press, AP, Corbis/Royalty-Free (background)

Contents

By reconstructing the Pan Am plane that exploded over Lockerbie, Scotland, in 1988, investigators determined where the bomb went off.

Chapter 1

What Happened at Lockerbie?

On December 21, 1988, Pan Am Flight 103, a passenger jet headed for New York City, blew up over the tiny town of Lockerbie, Scotland. An eyewitness watched from the ground: "[There] was a terrible explosion and the whole sky lit up. It was virtually raining fire—it was just liquid fire."[1] What was left of the jet plunged toward the earth and crashed onto the town, plowing through cars on the local highway. All 259 people on board were killed, 189 of them American. Eleven people on the ground were killed, too. The news shocked the world.[2]

Exactly what had happened? Was something wrong with the plane's fuel system? Or had the

The cockpit was the only intact piece found by investigators. They had to search the surrounding area to gather the remaining fragments.

explosion been caused by a bomb? An extensive investigation began at once. Agents from twenty-two law-enforcement agencies came to the crime scene. The Federal Bureau of Investigations (FBI) was one of the main agencies involved.

Pan Am 103 exploded at 31,000 feet in the air. One huge piece of the plane—the cockpit, where the pilots sit—was still in one piece when it hit the ground. Much of the aircraft and its cargo were in tiny pieces, however. Wind scattered the debris over a huge area. To figure out what happened, FBI special agents and other investigators had to search an area measuring about ten miles wide and eighty miles long.

Tom Thurman of the FBI's Explosives Unit will never forget the search. The investigators' instructions were simple: "If it's not growing, and it's not a rock, pick it up."[3] Very slowly, they went through fields. It seemed like they searched one blade of grass at a time. Some debris had fallen in thick woods. It had to be

> Bit by bit, investigators collected 200,000 pieces of evidence, including parts of the plane, passengers' belongings, and cargo.

located by spy satellites or investigators in helicopters. Bit by bit, investigators collected 200,000 pieces of evidence, including parts of the plane, passengers' belongings, and cargo.

Everything they collected was sent to Farnborough Royal Air Force Base outside London. Technicians took the pieces of the plane and started to rebuild it on a huge wire frame. By now, everybody had begun to think a bomb had caused this explosion.

Some of the evidence was sent to a crime lab. Investigators traveled the globe and interviewed people about many pieces of evidence. Once suspects were named and located, there would be other interviews to conduct. Eventually, investigators would do ten thousand interviews.

In the meantime, back in the lab, forensic scientists began to focus on a few key pieces of evidence. On the first day, an agent had found a piece of metal. An investigator realized it came from a luggage container—

A passenger had not
carried the bomb onto
the plane. It had been
put in a suitcase.

a big metal bin used to hold and transport suitcases. A chemist used a specialized tool to prove this piece of metal had traces of explosives on it.

The very next day, another piece of the same container was found. It also had leftover explosive material. Thurman remembers, "The odds against us finding those two pieces so fast can't be calculated. It can't happen. What was so important about it was that it told us that the bomb had been in the baggage area rather than the passenger cabin."[4] A passenger had not carried the bomb onto the plane. It had been put in a suitcase.

Eventually investigators put together more of the luggage container. They found out which pieces of luggage had been in the container. Finally, they figured out that the bomb had been in a Samsonite suitcase.

Then another clue caught the FBI's attention: one tiny piece of plastic no bigger than a thumbnail. An investigator concluded it was part of a circuit board from a Toshiba radio. The terrorists had hidden the bomb in this radio. The FBI figured out this model of radio was sold only in the Middle East. Now the investigators knew three things. They knew the size of the bomb. They knew it probably had been made in an Arab nation. Finally, they knew when and how it had gotten onto the plane.

The FBI's Director

The FBI is headed by a director. Until the 1970s, the U.S. attorney general appointed the FBI's director. Since then, the president has chosen the person for the job. The president's choice is then approved by the U.S. Senate. The FBI has not had many directors. This is because one man, J. Edgar Hoover (above), held the office for forty-eight years, from 1924 to 1972. In 1976, Congress limited the director's term to ten years.

PI/1353

PI/1232

PI/1806

PI/911

PK/2075

PK/1310A

PI/1808   PI/1807   PI/1803

PI/1388   PI/1420   PI/1431   PI/1466   PI/1487   PI/1488   PI/1538

PI/1545   PI/1548   PI/1552   PI/1564   PI/1565   PI/1589   PI/1590   PI/1591

PT/22

PI/1643   PI/1644   PT/24   PT/25   PT/68

PT/23

CMS   10   20

PP8932

A few bits of a gray shirt were the final clues that investigators needed to track down a suspect.

After that an English detective found a tiny piece of green circuit board. Thurman figured out that it came from inside a timer. He had found the bomb's timing mechanism. He learned that a Swiss company had sold twenty of these timers to Libya. The ruler of this African country had supported terrorists in the past. A timer just like this one had been used in another bomb planted by Libyans in Senegal.

A year after the crash, a final essential clue was found. One day, a Lockerbie resident went out to walk

> A year after the crash,
> a final essential clue
> was found by a man walking
> his dog.

his dog. He found a piece of gray fabric on a bush. Investigators had overlooked it. He turned it in. Technicians figured out that this shirt had been in the Samsonite suitcase along with the bomb. The shirt piece had a label. Detectives discovered the shirt had been made by a company on the island of Malta. They found the store on Malta that had sold this clothing.

The store owner knew exactly who had bought this particular shirt. It was an employee of the Libyan embassy, which was located just down the block from his store. The owner remembered the Libyan because he had purchased several pieces of clothing without

Today, the FBI counts
the Lockerbie case as
one of its greatest
successes.

caring what they looked like or what size they were. Intelligence—information secretly collected by law-enforcement officials or spies—revealed that the employee was a Libyan intelligence agent.

Finally, all the pieces fell into place. Authorities charged the man who had purchased the clothing, Abdel Basset Ali Al-Megrahi. They charged a second man, Lamen Khalifa Fhimah. Fhimah knew Megrahi and had worked at the Malta airport for Libyan Arab Airlines. Investigators thought Fhimah had put the Samsonite suitcase on an airplane. The United States concluded that the Libyan government had supported this act of terrorism. The U.S. government then placed sanctions, or punishments, against the country of Libya. All U.S. financial aid to the country stopped.

At first, the Libyan government refused to hand over the suspects. Finally, the United Nations convinced Libya to back down. The two men went to trial. In January 2001, Megrahi was found guilty and sentenced to life in prison. The jury found Fhimah innocent.[5] Today, the FBI counts the Lockerbie case as one of its greatest successes.

In April 2005, the Department of Homeland Security organized TOPOFF 3. This was the world's largest antiterror drill ever. FBI personnel were among the thousands of law-enforcement officers who took part.

TOPOFF 3 began when a small plane released simulated mustard gas in the sky over a busy waterfront in Connecticut. Nearby a car exploded into a real fireball. At the same time, a sprayer in an SUV began to release a fake biological weapon into a crowded neighborhood in New Jersey.

TOPOFF 3 participants did not know in advance what would happen. They sprang into action. Some worked the scenes of the "crimes." Others chased down "suspects." Medical personnel dealt with thousands of fake corpses and actors pretending to be wounded or ill. FBI agents practiced interviewing victims, collecting evidence, and arresting "terrorists." They took steps to prevent other attacks.

In the months that followed, federal officials went over what happened. They determined what the government would need to do better if chemical or biological weapons were really used against the United States. Two problems were immediately apparent. First, medical personnel became extremely tired. Second, participants showed a lack of experience with massive evacuations.[6] Now the government is putting in place better emergency plans. The FBI, for its part, continues to make preparedness training a high priority.

Since 1975, the FBI has had its headquarters in the J. Edgar Hoover Building on Pennsylvania Avenue near the White House in Washington, D.C. The building stands seven stories high in one section and eleven in another. It is built of poured concrete and looks like a huge rock box with a courtyard in the middle. The Hoover Building is an example of Brutalist architecture, a style originating in the 1950s and characterized by blockish, repetitive shapes.

Today the headquarters building is mostly filled with offices, including those of the FBI's most important staff members, such as the director. The FBI crime lab used to be in this building, but it recently moved to Quantico, Virginia.

In the past, the FBI offered visitors tours of its headquarters. It was a popular tour; half a million people

visited every year. Since September 11, the building has been closed to the public for security reasons. Security is extremely tight at the FBI headquarters. Guards are constantly on the watch for unauthorized people trying to enter the building.

Introducing the FBI

The Federal Bureau of Investigation is one of the best-known law-enforcement agencies in the world. It has more investigators than any other law-enforcement agency. Law-enforcement officers all over the world respect the FBI because of the extremely difficult work it does. The FBI solves challenging cases and prevents horrifying crimes, such as murder and kidnapping. To do so, it needs top-notch, intelligent, well-trained agents. It also needs the latest in high-tech tools and techniques. Other

Respected around the world, the FBI solves challenging cases and prevents horrifying crimes, such as murder and kidnapping.

law-enforcement agencies constantly ask the FBI to help with difficult cases.

The FBI is part of the U.S. Department of Justice. This crucial government department is responsible for upholding U.S. laws and is led by the attorney general. U.S. attorneys help the attorney general by representing the federal government in trials when a federal law has been broken. Federal laws are those passed by Congress, rather than by a state or local government. When a person breaks a federal law, he or she has committed a federal crime.

In 1949, a reporter asked an FBI agent who were the "toughest guys"—the criminals the Bureau would most like to capture.[7] This inspired FBI director J. Edgar Hoover to start supplying the news media with a list of the FBI's Ten Most Wanted Fugitives. The criminals on the Most Wanted List have broken the law many times. The list has included bank robbers, kidnappers, serial murderers, and drug lords. The agency believes the increased visibility of being on a poster will help agents find these people. Between 1950 and 2005, 480 people were placed on the Ten Most Wanted List. Four hundred fifty of them were eventually captured.

A television program called *America's Most Wanted*, hosted by John Walsh, has been on the air since 1988. It runs stories about people sought by and captured by the FBI and other law enforcement agencies. The FBI cooperates in the production of this television show.

Osama bin Laden was on the FBI's Most Wanted List in October 2005. (His name has been spelled different ways; on the FBI poster, it was spelled Usama bin Laden.) Victor Manuel Gerena was another name on that list. In 1983 he was accused of stealing $7 million from a company that provides building security. He stole the money after injecting two security guards with an unknown drug. Mobster James J. Bulger ran a notorious Boston crime gang that controlled many of the city's illegal drug sales. He is wanted on multiple murder charges. Robert William Fisher is accused of killing his wife and children before blowing up their house. The FBI tries to get the word out on these and other criminals to increase the chances that they will be caught.

FBI TEN MOST WANTED FUGITIVE

MURDER OF U.S. NATIONALS OUTSIDE THE UNITED STATES;
CONSPIRACY TO MURDER U.S. NATIONALS OUTSIDE THE UNITED STATES;
ATTACK ON A FEDERAL FACILITY RESULTING IN DEATH

USAMA BIN LADEN

Date of Photograph Unknown

Aliases: Usama Bin Muhammad Bin Ladin, Shaykh Usama Bin Ladin, the Prince, the Emir, Abu Abdallah, Mujahid Shaykh, Hajj, the Director

DESCRIPTION

Date of Birth:	1957	Hair:	Brown
Place of Birth:	Saudi Arabia	Eyes:	Brown
Height:	6' 4" to 6' 6"	Complexion:	Olive
Weight:	Approximately 160 pounds	Sex:	Male
Build:	Thin	Nationality:	Saudi Arabian
Occupation(s):	Unknown		
Remarks:	He is the leader of a terrorist organization known as Al-Qaeda "The Base." He walks with a cane.		

CAUTION

USAMA BIN LADEN IS WANTED IN CONNECTION WITH THE AUGUST 7, 1998, BOMBINGS OF THE UNITED STATES EMBASSIES IN DAR ES SALAAM, TANZANIA AND NAIROBI, KENYA. THESE ATTACKS KILLED OVER 200 PEOPLE.

CONSIDERED ARMED AND EXTREMELY DANGEROUS

IF YOU HAVE ANY INFORMATION CONCERNING THIS PERSON, PLEASE CONTACT YOUR LOCAL FBI OFFICE OR THE NEAREST U.S. EMBASSY OR CONSULATE.

REWARD

The United States Government is offering a reward of up to $5 million for information leading directly to the apprehension or conviction of Usama Bin Laden.

The FBI usually investigates these cases. There are a few federal offenses that are the responsibility of another agency. The Drug Enforcement Agency handles most drug cases, for example. The FBI, however, investigates violations of more than two hundred types of federal crimes. If a kidnapper takes a child from one state to another, it is a case for the FBI. FBI special agents handle some serial killer cases. They hunt down spies who have snuck into the United States to collect information about our military bases or high-tech companies.

FBI agents get involved in many nonviolent crimes. For example, the FBI is called when an official steals money from a government office. If someone creates a pirated movie or music recording to sell over the Internet, the FBI takes the case.

Since September 11, 2001, the FBI has devoted much more time to terrorism. Today the FBI's number-one priority is to prevent acts of terrorism by collecting information about terrorists and their plans and sharing it with other law-enforcement agencies.

Employing Thousands

As of March 31, 2006, the FBI had 30,430 employees. That number included 12,515 special agents, or investigators. The agency identifies the rest of its employees—who number 17,915—as support personnel.[8] These are people who assist the special agents in numerous ways. Some support jobs are filled by specialists, like crime-lab scientists. One very important group of

On the Job

Eight thousand FBI employees work at the agency's headquarters in Washington, D.C. What about the rest of the roughly thirty thousand employees? Hundreds report to work in Quantico, Virginia. This is where the FBI's crime lab and training facilities are located. The rest work in other FBI offices. As of 2005, the FBI had offices in close to five hundred American cities. There were fifty-six field offices in big cities and four hundred satellite offices in smaller cities. In 2005, the FBI also had fifty main offices and ten smaller offices located in foreign countries. It expected to have a total of eighty offices outside of the United States by 2007.[9]

specialists is the FBI's intelligence analysts. These are the people who collect information about criminals—especially terrorists.[10]

The agency also employs a huge number of people without advanced training. These people include secretaries, carpenters, maintenance workers, and many more. Analysts and agents could not do their jobs without people in support positions.

A variety of exciting work is available at the FBI. The agency employs people from all kinds of backgrounds, with many types of experience and education. This book introduces readers to the types of jobs available at the FBI. It also suggests ways to prepare for them.

Former FBI Director J. Edgar Hoover (left) brings gangster Louis "Lepke" Buchalter (center) to court in 1940. The FBI has been investigating organized crime since the 1920s.

Chapter 2

A Short History of the FBI

Most Americans would probably be surprised to learn that the FBI was not founded until 1908. Of course, crime has been a problem in the United States for far more than one hundred years. For a long time, however, local and state police forces were the ones that investigated crime. There were not as many federal laws in the past as there are now. Other than counterfeiting—printing fake money—there were not many crimes committed against the federal government.

The Secret Service was formed in 1865 to investigate counterfeiting. After President William McKinley was assassinated in 1901, the Secret Service's number-one priority and main responsibility became protecting the president of the United States. However, Secret Service agents still did some work for the Department of Justice, such as investigating mail robbery.

Then, in 1906, large-scale land fraud began to occur. President Theodore Roosevelt became angry when he learned that cheaters were claiming government land that was supposed to go to settlers. He ordered the Department of Justice to open a government investigation. At first the department used Secret Service agents. However, soon Congress passed a new law that prohibited other federal government agencies from borrowing Secret Service agents. Attorney General Charles Bonaparte and President Roosevelt agreed it was time for the Department of Justice to have its own investigators. This force grew to become the modern FBI.

The Bureau of Investigation Begins

At first, only thirty-one investigators worked for the Department of Justice.[1] In 1909, the attorney general named this force the Bureau of Investigation. By 1914, the Bureau had an office in Washington. It also had one agent each in thirty large cities.[2]

That same year, World War I (1914–1918) broke out. Germany and Austria fought on one side. Great Britain, France, and Russia fought on the other. At first, Americans tried not to become involved in the war. In 1917, as the end of the war neared, the United States entered on the side of Great Britain. During the war, the Bureau of Investigation grew in importance. Its agents were assigned new responsibilities, such as hunting for spies. They tried to prevent sabotage by keeping U.S. enemies from damaging submarines or weapons factories.

Hoover Takes Command

In 1924, the Bureau of Investigation entered a new era. The attorney general appointed a young man named J. Edgar Hoover as its new director. Hoover made some positive changes at the Bureau. He decided that agents

J. Edgar Hoover served as director of the Bureau for almost fifty years.

would be hired and promoted for their skills, not because a politician recommended them. He made sure the agency kept good records and started its fingerprint file. Over time, though, Hoover would receive criticism. One reason was that he had the agency collect information about people he did not like. These people included the nation's great civil-rights leaders. Hoover also was accused of blackmail. Still, he remained in command of the Bureau until his death in 1972.

Gangsters

By the mid-1920s, the Bureau of Investigation turned its focus to gangsters. In 1920, the Eighteenth Amendment

Catching Gangsters

The 1920s and 1930s were a time of peak activity for gangsters. FBI agents were in on many of the most famous gangster chases.

On February 14, 1929, members of Al Capone's mob put on stolen police uniforms. They cornered seven members of a rival Chicago gang and killed them with machine guns.

FBI agent Eliot Ness (left) worked for years to put Al Capone behind bars.

to the U.S. Constitution went into effect. It prohibited Americans from making, buying, selling, or drinking alcohol. Reformers hoped this would make the United States a better place to live. Instead, a crime wave developed.

Bootleggers began to make large supplies of alcohol. Smugglers transported liquor over the border from Canada and Mexico. Organized crime—crime

This event went down in history as the St. Valentine's Day Massacre.

In court, Capone's doctor said he could not possibly have been involved in the shooting. He swore Capone was sick in bed in Miami at the time. FBI agents proved that Capone had been seen at Miami's race tracks. His alibi was false.[3]

During the same era, the Bureau tracked down infamous gangster Machine Gun Kelly. Agents investigated the 1933 kidnapping of millionaire Charles F. Urschel in Oklahoma. Urschel's family paid a ransom demand of $200,000, and he was released.

When agents interviewed him about the kidnapping, Urschel recalled hearing an airplane fly overhead every morning and every night. He remembered that on one particular day it rained and there was no flight. Agents used this information to figure out which airfield he had been near. Next to the field they found a house connected to gangster Machine Gun Kelly.

Charles Lindbergh was an international celebrity, known for his flying adventures. The kidnapping and murder of his son in 1932 shocked the nation.

that is coordinated by a group like a gang—came into being. Gangsters were involved in buying and selling liquor, bank robberies, and other crimes. Over time, the Bureau of Investigation started to pursue famous gangsters like Al "Scarface" Capone and Baby Face Nelson.

The Lindbergh Case

In the mid-1930s, the Bureau of Investigation gained fame after it cracked the Lindbergh baby kidnapping case. Charles Lindbergh became an American hero when he made the first solo nonstop flight across the

> The Lindbergh family had paid the kidnapper a huge ransom in what were known as gold certificates.

Atlantic Ocean in 1927. In 1932 Lindbergh's young son was kidnapped and found dead two months later. Americans were shocked.

At first the Bureau of Investigation was not in on the case. It took over after Congress authorized it to investigate kidnappings that took victims across state borders. The Lindbergh family had paid the kidnapper a huge ransom in what were known as gold certificates. Several times, one of the gold certificates was spent. Investigators got descriptions of the man who was spending them. His accent matched the one described by the man who had dropped off the ransom. Bureau investigators suspected that the kidnapper lived in the Bronx. They gave a list of the gold certificates' serial numbers to gas stations in New York.

By this time, the U.S. Treasury had stopped issuing gold certificates. They were not often seen, so their use was noticeable. In 1934, a gas-station attendant was paid with one of the Lindbergh certificates. He notified the Bureau of Investigation and gave them a license-plate number. The Bureau traced it to a German immigrant named Bruno Hauptmann. A handwriting analyst got a sample of Hauptmann's writing and compared it with the ransom note. He concluded that Hauptmann wrote the note. Other agents went to Hauptmann's home and found other incriminating evidence. This evidence was presented during what was called the trial of the century. Hauptmann was found guilty and sentenced to death. Hoover expressed great pride in his agents' work.

A New Name

By the mid-1930s, the Bureau of Investigation had begun to earn an impressive reputation as the law-enforcement agency that would "always get its man." Machine Gun Kelly, one of the toughest gangsters of the 1920s and 1930s, called the FBI agents who arrested him G-men, meaning Government Men. In 1935 James Cagney made a movie called *G Men*. This pleased Hoover. From that point on, the phrase was well

Because of the Bureau's work, Bruno Hauptmann (front, center) was found guilty of kidnapping and killing the Lindbergh baby.

known. Under Hoover's orders, G-men always worked in a suit and tie. In the public eye they were not just smart and tough, but also glamorous.

Also in 1935, the Bureau's name was changed to the Federal Bureau of Investigation. The next year, Europe was swept by political unrest. This would lead to World War II (1939–1945). In this conflict, allies Germany, Italy, and Japan fought against the old alliance of Great Britain, France, the Soviet Union, and the United States. President Franklin D. Roosevelt asked the FBI to track down subversives—people suspected to be working against the U.S. government. Agents investigated members of the German-American Bund, an organization formed by Germans who lived in the United States and supported the Nazis. The FBI also investigated communists. They also searched again for spies and saboteurs.[4]

Enemies from the Inside

After World War II ended, the United States and the Soviet Union became enemies. Government officials learned that the Soviet Union had learned U.S. atomic bomb secrets, so agents resumed their hunt for spies. FBI evidence led to the arrest of Ethel and Julius Rosenberg. Julius was an electrical engineer who had worked for the U.S. Army. He and his wife were accused of giving American secrets to the Soviet Union. These spies were sentenced to death in 1951.

By this time, the nation was in the middle of the Second Red Scare, a time when many Americans were afraid that Communists (nicknamed Reds) were in their midst and might try to take over the American government. The first time America experienced a Red Scare had been after the Russian Revolution in 1917. It lasted until 1920. The Second Red Scare would last from 1947 to 1954. It began when communism once more began to spread around the world. Some government

The FBI and the CIA

Many people get confused about the difference between the FBI and another government agency called the Central Intelligence Agency (CIA). The CIA is separate from the FBI. It is an intelligence agency, not a law-enforcement agency. This means its job is to collect information about foreign governments, organizations, and individuals—including terrorists. The CIA is not supposed to collect information about U.S. citizens. CIA agents do not arrest criminals as FBI agents do. The CIA sends its information to other intelligence agencies, to the FBI, and to other countries' law-enforcement agencies.

officials believed Soviets were running the American Communist Party. They thought communists planned to infiltrate American government. Many Americans saw communism as a threat to a democratic way of life.

From 1956 to 1971, Hoover made hunting down subversives one of the FBI's major goals. He established a counterintelligence program called Cointelpro. Cointelpro agents used hidden surveillance methods— including wiretaps and break-ins—to watch the activities of communists. During the 1960s agents also spied on civil-rights activists such as Dr. Martin Luther King, Jr. Hoover also ordered agents to keep files on the activities of people against the Vietnam War.

Over time, the American public became aware of Cointelpro's activities. People began to question whether the FBI was overstepping its bounds. They believed it was wrong to investigate people who disagreed with the government, rather than people who actually wanted to bring down the government.

In 1972, Hoover died in his sleep. Within a short time, Congress began the Watergate hearings. These hearings led to the discovery that President Richard M. Nixon had ordered aides to break into offices of the Democratic Party. Over time, it would become clear that the FBI helped cover up Nixon's actions. However, one FBI man, known as Deep Throat, helped reporters discover the truth. In 2005 Deep Throat was revealed to be W. Mark Felt. Many Americans see Felt as a hero.

A New Focus

By the mid-1970s, the FBI's reputation was harmed. Many Americans distrusted the agency. Its reputation improved, however, as the agency turned its focus away from the hunt for people who disagreed with the government. In the 1980s, FBI agents had many espionage (spying) cases to solve. First they caught John Walker. With a small group of other people, Walker had been selling U.S. Navy secrets to the Soviet Union since 1967. The FBI also tracked down another spy named Robert Pelton. While working for the National Security Administration, Pelton had sold secret information to the Russians.

Agents also began to focus more attention on white-collar crime such as public corruption. In the

W. Mark Felt poses for a 1958 newspaper story. Felt later claimed that he was Deep Throat, the anonymous source who leaked secrets about Watergate.

Abscam or Abdul Scam scandal, FBI agents set up a sting operation. An agent pretended to be a fictitious Arab sheik named Abdul. He offered bribes to several U.S. congressmen in exchange for secret information. Other agents caught the congressmen accepting the bribes. In addition to corruption, the FBI began to focus on drug trafficking—the transport and sale of illegal drugs. An even bigger focus would be terrorism.

The FBI's Most Wanted Terrorists List

After September 11, 2001, the FBI started to publicize a Most Wanted Terrorists List as well as its Ten Most Wanted Fugitives List. In September 2005, there were eighteen men on the Terrorists List. All were Arab, and all were wanted in connection with attacks on the United States or on American citizens abroad. Osama bin Laden topped the list. The FBI removes people from the list only after they are captured or proved dead.

Terrorism

It was in the 1970s that the FBI first began fighting terrorists. Terrorists are people who use violence to try to disrupt a government. Some Americans believe this is a new problem. In fact, terrorism began in ancient history. Some terrorists have acted because they are angry about the Jewish occupation of Israel after World War II. Palestinians had lived on this land for hundreds of years.

Today many terrorists are driven by a belief that Israel should be returned to Arab rule. Not all terrorists have acted on this belief, however. In the middle of the nineteenth century, many colonies began to seek independence. The Irish, for example, fought hard to throw off British rule. In some cases, terrorists began to fight for these causes. In fact, World War I began after a Serbian terrorist assassinated the Austrian archduke.

A new era in terrorism began in the late 1960s. There was a rash of hijackings, when terrorists took over airplanes and took their passengers hostage. Most of these terrorists wanted to force a government to free other members of their group from prison. In 1972 Palestinian terrorists kidnapped and killed eleven members of the Israeli Olympic team.

The FBI worked on all of the major terrorism investigations involving American citizens. In 1984 the agency was in charge of security at the Los Angeles Olympics. Agents worked hard to make sure the events of 1972 would not be repeated. In 1986, Congress gave the FBI authority over terrorist acts committed against American citizens outside the United States. By the mid-1990s, the FBI was spending a huge amount of its time and effort on terrorism. The FBI spearheaded investigations into the World Trade Center bombing of 1993 and the bombing of

The bin Laden Task Force

The FBI has been paying attention to Osama bin Laden for more than ten years. Retired agent Dan Coleman started to study Islamic extremists after the 1993 attack on the World Trade Center. Bin Laden's name started to come up. At first he was mistakenly thought to be a dilettante—just a wealthy playboy. By 1996, the FBI and the CIA had formed a joint task force charged with finding bin Laden. As of 2006, they were still searching.[5]

Oklahoma City's federal building in 1995. By September 11, 2001, the FBI was already searching for Osama bin Laden. Intelligence officers recognized him as a dangerous terrorist leader.

The New FBI

The FBI got a new director, Robert Mueller, just days before September 11, 2001. When he came into office,

The FBI caught Timothy J. McVeigh, one of the men responsible for the Oklahoma City bombing. Agents lead McVeigh away from an Oklahoma courthouse after being charged in the attack in April 1995.

Mueller thought his chief concern was going to be updating the FBI's computer system. Then terrorists flew four airplanes straight into New York City's World

After the September 11 terror attacks, the FBI launched a massive investigation into uncovering the identities of the hijackers.

Trade Center, the Pentagon in Washington, D.C., and a field in southwestern Pennsylvania. Everything changed after September 11. The FBI launched a massive investigation into the identities of the hijackers. President George W. Bush asked the FBI to change its mission.

Today the FBI has a new priority list. Its first job is to defend the United States from terrorist attacks. It also protects the United States from foreign intelligence operations and espionage, or spying.

The FBI protects the United States from cyber and high-tech crime. This means it tries to stop attacks using computer systems and other technology. The Bureau is especially concerned with attacks on government computer networks and identity theft.

The FBI also combats public corruption at all levels. This means it works to ensure that government officials

The FBI investigated the September 11 crash sites, including where the World Trade Center towers once stood.

do not cheat or steal. The agency protects Americans' civil rights by fighting hate crimes. It also investigates criminal organizations, such as the Mafia.

The agency continues to handle major white-collar crime, such as stealing millions of dollars from a company. It also fights violent crime, such as murder and rape. It helps out many different kinds of law-enforcement agencies. Some are other federal agencies, like U.S. Customs and Border Protection. Others are at the state, county, and city levels. It assists other countries' police and investigators when they need it. Finally, the Bureau works to upgrade its technology. FBI workers are constantly inventing new high-tech equipment that helps agents fight crime.

Throughout its history, the FBI has grown. It changes constantly. As a result, FBI jobs also have changed. This is one of the most exciting things about working at the FBI—there is always a new challenge ahead.

As a part of their training, FBI special agents learn how to use different types of firearms and how to handle challenging situations.

Chapter 3

Agents at Work

The FBI is a huge organization with about thirty thousand employees. The FBI is actually not the largest federal law-enforcement agency. The largest is U.S. Customs and Border Protection, which is in charge of controlling who and what comes into the United States. The FBI does, however, have more investigators than any other law-enforcement agency on the entire planet. Its investigators are called special agents.

What Are Special Agents Like?

In some ways, special agents are all the same. Their jobs require them to be intelligent and observant. They must be able to pay attention to detail, enjoy problem solving, and keep organized records. FBI employees also must be

Cold Cases

One of the most frustrating parts of being a special agent is being unable to solve a case. When agents run out of clues to follow, cases became "cold." In recent years, agents have solved cases that seemed impossible to solve. One was the case of the Unabomber. This mystery criminal sent his first bomb through the mail in 1978. The FBI searched for him for seventeen years. In 1995 the Unabomber demanded that newspapers publish a letter that he called a manifesto. It explained what he thought was wrong with the United States. Two newspapers agreed to publish the letter. They hoped it would help in the search. It worked. Theodore Kaczynski's brother recognized his brother's ideas and turned him in. Kaczynski was arrested in 1996.

In 2005 the anthrax case was in grave danger of going cold. Someone had sent anthrax, a deadly disease, through the mail to news agencies and government offices in 2001. Five people died, and twenty-two people got sick. Special teams were needed to handle the infected materials (right). Thirty special agents worked the case until 2004. Trying to solve the mystery, agents had traveled all over the globe to conduct eight thousand interviews. In 2005 the FBI admitted that it was running out of leads. It cut the number of agents assigned to the case to twenty-one.[1]

Many people hope the FBI will solve the cold case of Emmitt Till. In 1955 Emmitt, a fourteen-year-old

African-American boy, was murdered. He had been accused of whistling at a white woman.[2] The public's outrage at Emmitt's death has lasted for decades.

The FBI often takes over cold cases from other law-enforcement agencies. It is able to solve some of these cases.[3] It is most successful when there is DNA or an unidentified fingerprint available.

good at keeping secrets. Cases can take a long time to crack, so special agents must be patient and determined. Also, special agents must have a true respect for the law and the ability to follow instructions and guidelines.

Special agents are investigators. They spend most of their time doing what you might think of as detective work—following leads, searching for clues or evidence, and building a case against criminals. What they investigate varies from day to day and from case to case.

Special agents are encouraged to specialize in one type of crime. However, the FBI makes sure special agents get a variety of assignments. Especially when agents are starting out, they will be asked to work on different sorts of investigations. This helps them learn new skills and find out exactly what they like to do. It also means that the agency will have plenty of people to assign to large cases, no matter what the specialty.

Agents need to know how to gather evidence. They go to crime scenes and interview witnesses or suspects. Sometimes they go through documents or records to search for evidence of a crime. Sometimes they have to go undercover—to put on a disguise and to create a fake name and history. Other times the agents undertake surveillance—watching people and places. It is important for special agents to keep track of what they have found out. This means report writing is a constant part of their job. Special agents pass their findings on to U.S. attorneys. The attorneys decide whether criminal charges should be filed, whether arrests should be made, and how trials should be conducted. Special agents sometimes have to help prepare cases for trial. They appear at trials as witnesses.

At any one time, special agents are working on hundreds of types of cases. The agency is responsible for investigating violations of about 250 federal laws. There are always agents conducting investigations into terrorist activity. They hope to find new terrorists or to bring down a terrorist organization.[4]

Squads

Special agents are organized into squads. Different offices have different squads. Special agents' squad assignments can change from time to time. One type of squad handles applicant review. These agents check the backgrounds of people who apply for White House jobs, for example.

Members of computer-crime squads track down hackers—people who try to break into computer networks. These criminals may hope to steal valuable information, such as credit-card numbers or financial data. Others want to cause a network to crash, which can create chaos.

Members of counterterrorism squads try both to prevent terrorism and to investigate acts of terrorism. This often requires cooperation with other federal law-enforcement agencies. Environmental crime squads check out illegal dumping—the illegal disposal of dangerous materials or hazardous waste. Homicide squads investigate murders. Members of the Hostage Rescue Team try to free people who have been captured by criminals.

On the Case

What are some cases special agents have worked on over the last few years? They range from big to small. Some FBI cases are in the newspapers day after day, but the public never hears about most of them.

In August 2005, agents arrested four terrorists who had been planning attacks in California. A leader

---

Members of a terrorist cell went online to choose targets. They planned to bomb California military bases, among other sites.

---

of a radical Muslim organization had made the plan while he was in the California State Prison. The man's goal was to kill what he called infidels, especially Jews and supporters of the nation of Israel. His followers—members of his terrorist cell—went online to choose targets. They planned to bomb California military bases, an Israeli consulate building, airplanes belonging to an Israeli airline, and Jewish synagogues (places of worship) in and around Los Angeles.

Members of the FBI's Hazardous Materials Response Unit investigate the famous anthrax case in Boca Raton, Florida.

The men had already scoped out their targets. They held up a dozen gas stations and stole money to buy the materials they needed. They purchased shotguns and practiced using them. They planned to attack synagogues on religious holidays and to kill as many people as possible.

No one in law enforcement had a clue about the terrorists' plans. Then two of the men were arrested in connection with one of the gas-station holdups. Several police officers from Torrance and Los Angeles realized the robbers were planning something bigger. They contacted the FBI's Joint Terrorism Task Force in Los Angeles. The agents went to work to discover who else might be involved in the plans. Then they made the arrests.[5]

In another case that made headlines, the FBI helped track down terrorists outside of the United States. These people had plotted the 1998 bombings of U.S. embassies in Tanzania and Kenya. In a less famous case, the FBI arrested a British citizen who was accused of bringing missiles into the United States.[6]

The FBI is constantly searching for spies. In 1994, an employee of the CIA was arrested for passing secrets to the Soviet Union. At that point, the FBI took the CIA's cue and began to look for a traitor inside its own offices. By 2000, the FBI focused on a special agent named Robert Philip Hanssen. The FBI learned that Hanssen had begun selling U.S. secrets to the Soviet Union in 1986. Special agents hacked into

Special agents leave the house of Robert Hanssen, an FBI agent who was convicted of spying for the Soviet Union.

his computer and entered his car and office to find evidence. Finally, they arrested him in the act of passing along secret information. In 2002, Hanssen was sentenced to life in prison.[7]

Some cases require the FBI to cooperate with foreign law-enforcement agencies as well as other American agencies. One of these cases took place in 2003. The National Science Foundation (NSF) maintains a research station at the South Pole. One day in May, its staff received an anonymous e-mail stating that a hacker had gained access to NSF's computer system. The NSF simply could not afford to have its computer system shut down. At that time of year, the South Pole is in the dead of winter. Except in an extreme emergency, planes cannot land there. The computer is the only link between the station's staff and the outside world. Special agents found out that e-mails sent in reply to the hackers were being read in an Internet café in far-off Romania. Romanian police flushed them out.[8]

Protecting Art

Many people do not know that the FBI has an art-theft program. It is designed to catch art thieves who take paintings, sculptures, or cultural artifacts from one country to another. In one case, special agents recovered a rare and valuable piece of armor for the country of Peru. The piece is called a backflap, and was worn by a ruler almost two thousand years ago. The

The FBI found the hackers that broke into the computer systems of the NSF's Amundsen-Scott South Station at the South Pole in 2003.

Special agents recovered a
piece of ancient armor for
the country of Peru.

backflap was stolen when tomb raiders broke into a royal tomb in 1987. Special agents became involved in 1997, when a smuggler tried to sell the backflap. Undercover agents posed as potential buyers. Two suspects were charged with smuggling. One was tried and sentenced. The other escaped arrest and is still at large. The armor has been returned to Peru. It is now housed in a museum.[9]

Feeling Proud

Special agents often feel proud when they work on an especially important case. Dan O'Brien heads up the FBI's Public Corruption and Government Fraud Program. He talked about a time when twenty-six employees of the Arizona Department of Motor Vehicles issued fake driver's licenses and ID cards in exchange for bribes. Such a case might not seem serious at first, he pointed out. Maybe some teenagers just wanted fake IDs to buy beer. Think again. "What if it's a terrorist trying to get one of those licenses?" O'Brien asked.[10] Being an FBI agent is not just about excitement. It is about making sure American citizens stay safe.

What Is It Like to Be a Special Agent?

FBI special agents work all over the United States and all over the world. Some agents get assigned to FBI headquarters in Washington, D.C. Most agents work for the agency's field offices, satellite offices (smaller offices that report to field offices), or attaché offices, which are located in foreign countries. Egypt, China, and Italy are just a few examples. In some cases, field offices are responsible for a large area. Other offices have responsibility for a small area with a large population.

Montana does not have its own field office. Neither does Idaho. The Salt Lake City, Utah, office has authority over all cases in Montana, Idaho, and Utah. The Minneapolis, Minnesota, office covers cases in Minnesota, North Dakota, and South Dakota. Alaska has just one field office. California has four. The biggest field offices are in New York, Los Angeles, and Washington, D.C. Washington's field office is separate from the FBI headquarters. Field offices are supported by satellite offices, which are in smaller cities. For example, the FBI field office in Los Angeles has ten satellite offices.

All special agents get assigned to one office. They generally spend a short time each day in their office unless their case requires them to travel. At the office they check in and catch up on paperwork. Office locations vary greatly from place to place. In some cities, field offices are located in government buildings with other federal offices. In other places, an FBI field office gets a building of its own. Individual offices also vary. Some agents work in big open areas called bullpens, while others get a private office. In general, satellite offices have less room than field offices. Sometimes the FBI transfers agents from one office to another.

Sometimes agents work alone. More often, they work on teams. The FBI often helps out in other law-enforcement agencies' investigations. Many special

Special agents have to be prepared to chase criminals and sometimes face extreme danger.

agents are asked to join task forces or discussion groups focused on crime.

FBI special agents' jobs can be extremely demanding. Few agents ever work what Americans consider a regular workweek—Monday through Friday from 8:00 A.M. to 5:00 P.M. Agents often have to work a fifty-hour week. The agency recently started to let some special agents work part-time, however. This is one way to hold on to experienced special agents who have a family. All agents know that they are always on call. They carry cell phones and pagers with them at all times in case they are needed at a moment's notice.

A special agent's job is exciting, but it can be difficult. Special agents must be in top physical condition. They have to be prepared to chase criminals trying to make a getaway. Also, their jobs can be mentally stressful. When a crime makes the news, agents are under great pressure to solve a case. They experience frustration when a criminal gets away or they cannot find the evidence they need. Special agents sometimes face extreme danger.

For all its difficulties, a special-agent job can be very rewarding. Most agents greatly enjoy their work. They like the variety. They enjoy the pride they feel when they crack a tough case. They like the respect they get from the public. Many agents think the FBI has a positive work environment. Special agents protect one another in dangerous situations, and they often form strong friendships. Many retired agents become active in former special-agent associations.[11]

Another good part of the job is the pay. Special agents are among the best paid of all law-enforcement officers. In 2006, special agent base salaries started at $43,441 per year. In addition to their regular salary, special agents were paid one-quarter more. This extra money is called availability pay. Agents earn extra because they have to be on call at all times and they often work overtime. In expensive cities, special agents receive more pay than those who work in areas with a lower cost of living.

Special agents' salaries automatically increase over time. Once they have been on the job for a while, special agents can apply for promotion. They might become a supervisor or a manager. Supervisors' salaries start at around $100,000 per year.[12]

All FBI employees get generous benefits. They get vacation time, sick leave, and health and life insurance. Special agents retire after twenty years of service. The law requires them to retire by age fifty-seven unless they get special permission to work longer. Retired agents receive a generous pension.

Qualifications

There are several qualifications for the job of special agent. Agents must be U.S. citizens. Applicants must be between twenty-three and thirty-seven years old. All applicants must have a degree from a four-year college or university. It does not matter what their major was at college. A degree in law or law enforcement is helpful, but the agency even considers English majors. It is most important for future FBI staff to take courses that develop research and analytical skills.

Women and people of color are especially encouraged to apply for special-agent jobs. In the past, the FBI and other law-enforcement agencies have been accused of discrimination. Today the agency recognizes the need for a diverse workforce. In 2005, readers of *Careers and the Disabled* magazine ranked the FBI as the best government agency for which to work.[13]

Special-agent applicants must qualify for one of five programs. The agency considers people with a law degree for the law program. People with a bachelor's degree in accounting are invited to apply for the accounting entry program.

The agency needs more people who speak foreign languages. Its special language entry program is open to people who speak one of the languages the FBI needs. In 2005, the agency was especially interested in hiring people who speak Spanish,

---

The FBI needs more people who speak foreign languages, especially Spanish, Arabic, French, Farsi, and Mandarin.

Arabic, French, Farsi, or Mandarin.[14] Applicants to the language entry program have to pass a test on listening comprehension, reading comprehension, and translation.

In 2005, the agency added a new information-technology program for people with expertise in computer science or electrical engineering. In 2006, the agency began actively recruiting people to fill its information-technology positions. It especially needed system engineers to test new computer systems and data engineers to work on its databases.[15] There is also a diversified program for applicants who lack one of the specialties mentioned earlier. Applicants to the diversified program must have a college degree, as well as three years of work experience or an advanced degree plus two years of work experience.

In addition to quick minds, all special agents need fit bodies. The agency has weight criteria. This means it checks to see if applicants' height and weight are balanced. For example, women who are 5 feet, 6 inches tall should weigh between 114 and 161 pounds. The agency also has body-fat requirements. Men's body fat must be less than 19 percent of their total weight. Women's body fat should make up less than 22 percent of their weight. These requirements are important because the job can be physically demanding. FBI recruiters point out that being in shape—being able to run, jump, or fight—saves agents' lives.

Every applicant is given a thorough background check. Applicants are dismissed right away for any of the

Steven Gomez, one of several Latino agents with the FBI, answers questions about a national antiterrorism campaign in 2004. The FBI wants more women and minorities to join the agency.

following reasons: "the use of drugs, bad credit, failure of drug test, past criminal arrest, lack of candor [honesty or openness], polygraph [lie-detector test] failure, falsifying information, [and] default on government student loans."[16] All applicants must be willing to relocate and to be on call at all times.

Applying

The FBI constantly accepts applications for special agents. Although it is possible to apply for a job in person at a field office, the best way is to apply online.

The application process has many steps. First, human-resources personnel review applications to make sure applicants qualify for the job. They then

```
Applicants go through a
background check. The FBI
     interview applicants'
families, friends, neighbors,
     and coworkers.
```

weigh applicants' qualifications. People with the best qualifications are asked to take some tests. The first test is called the Biographical Data Inventory. It measures specific abilities, like a person's ability to organize. The questions look like this:

S1. In connection with your work, in which of the following have you taken the most pride?

A. Having been able to avoid any major controversies.
B. Having gotten where you are on your own.
C. Having been able to work smoothly with people.

D. Having provided a lot of new ideas, good or bad.

E. Having been able to do well whatever management has requested.[17]

The second test measures cognitive ability—a person's ability to solve math problems and to understand charts and graphs. The Situational Judgment Test finds out whether the applicant has good judgment and can handle a crisis. A sample question from this test asks what you would do if you saw a man robbing a store. Would you:

A. Leave the store as quickly as possible and call the police.

B. Try to apprehend the robber yourself.

C. Follow the man and call the police as soon as he appears settled somewhere.

D. Do nothing, as you do not wish to get involved in the matter.

Finally, people applying for foreign-language jobs take two tests in reading, listening, and speaking.

Applicants who pass their tests are asked to fill out a longer application form. Then they are considered for an interview. If the interview goes well, applicants go through a background check. This is a tough process. The FBI checks applicants' credit and arrest records. They also double-check every applicant's educational record.[18] They interview applicants' families, friends, neighbors, and coworkers to find out as much information as possible.

Before the process is completed, applicants have to get a clean bill of health from a doctor. They must be able to pass a fitness test. This test includes sit-ups, push-ups, a sprint, and a run of 1.5 miles. The entire application process takes several months.

Training

Once they get the job, special agents report to the FBI Academy for training. The academy is located in Quantico, Virginia. Until recently, training took sixteen weeks. However, as special agents' responsibilities have

---

In the classroom, agents study the law and the history of terrorism and organized crime. They also take classes on how to interview witnesses and suspects.

---

expanded to include more intelligence work, the FBI changed the training period to eighteen weeks. All new recruits get 708 hours of instruction.

Some training is done in classrooms. The academy's curriculum includes many different courses. New agents study the law. They take classes on the history of terrorism and organized crime. They practice their communication skills and learn how to interview suspects and witnesses. There are classes about forensic science, criminal behavior, and ethics.

Hogan's Alley

At the FBI Academy in Quantico, Virginia, there is a mock city named Hogan's Alley. New recruits go there to practice so they will be prepared for real-life situations. The FBI hires actors to help with the training. The actors pose as criminals, suspects, witnesses, and victims. They stage crimes such as bank robberies, kidnappings, or assaults on an agent—all to test how recruits handle different challenges. In Hogan's Alley, special agents learn to conduct surveillance, to make an arrest, and to avoid getting shot or killed. The agents get a chance to try out their weapons, vehicles, radios, and surveillance equipment.

At the FBI Academy, agents take classes in several subjects, including law and criminology.

Agents also get special training in firearms. They learn how to handle handguns, shotguns, and carbines (a type of rifle). They practice target shooting. They learn not only how to shoot a suspect, but also how to protect themselves from getting shot when under fire. Agents also learn about gun safety and how to take care of their weapons.

Special Agent

In physical-training classes, agents do exercises. They run every day. They also take defense training, such as the martial art of judo. This will help them if they need to fight a suspect hand-to-hand. Agents push their bodies to perform even when they are very tired, angry, or scared.

New agents also take special driving classes. They learn some new driving techniques in the classroom. Then they head out to a special track to practice their

---

Agents push their bodies
to perform even when
they are very tired,
angry, or scared.

---

techniques behind the wheel. They learn what to do in case of skidding. They also learn how to avoid dangers quickly. All this prepares them for high-speed car chases.[19]

Trainees describe their time at Quantico as difficult but fun. Later on, special agents return there periodically for new training to update their skills. The FBI also provides more training in offices around the country. Some training is one-on-one with a mentor. Other times agents gather to watch videos or to participate in a teleconference. Some continuing education occurs as distance learning over the Internet.

Weapons

Special agents have carried handguns since 1934. For a long time, all agents were issued a .38 caliber revolver. Then they started to carry semiautomatics. These guns have a magazine clip that holds ammunition. Semiautomatics are also lighter and carry more bullets. Over the last few years, the FBI has changed which semiautomatic its agents use. For a short time, they carried 10-millimeter pistols. These were too powerful, so the agency started to issue Smith and Wesson's .40. Today many agents use a Glock model.

Field offices also supply rifles for agents' use. Rifles have longer barrels than semiautomatics. SWAT teams use rifles when agents cannot get close to a suspect. Agents also use concussion grenades, which make a huge amount of noise.

At the FBI Academy, all recruits learn how to carry and clean a gun. They learn to shoot at a target. Once they graduate, special agents are tested on their shooting skills four times a year. The FBI also trains law-enforcement personnel from other agencies how to use weapons.[20]

On the Job

After graduating from the FBI Academy, special agents start a probationary period of two years. This means they are being tested to make sure they can do the job well. After September 11, 2001, the FBI changed how its career path works. In the past, agents were assigned to a specific field office and a

> In the past, agents were assigned to a specific field office and a squad. Today all agents are asked to develop a speciality.

squad. Today all agents are asked to develop a specialty, such as intelligence (collecting information about suspected criminals), counterintelligence (preventing spies from getting secret information that could damage the country's security), cyber crime, or general criminal activity.

Before they specialize, new agents rotate through a variety of jobs. This ensures they have a wide range of experience. Everybody's first assignment lasts for three years at a small field office. Special agents receive broad training with a focus on intelligence. After three years, agents transfer to a larger field office and begin to specialize.

Surveillance Equipment

The FBI uses a variety of equipment to observe suspects secretly. Some equipment lets agents watch suspects from afar. Night-vision goggles greatly increase light so agents can watch suspects in the dark. Eavesdropping equipment lets agents listen in on conversations from a great distance. Bugs pick up sound and send it to a remote receiver over radio waves. The FBI has wiretapped suspects' phone lines for decades. This allows agents to listen in on their phone calls. Today a new type of wiretapping lets agents read suspects' e-mails and instant messages.[21] The FBI has eighty aircraft equipped with cameras and eavesdropping equipment. Agents use the equipment to gather information from the air.[22] FBI agents use satellites to monitor phone calls around the world. They listen for key words and phrases such as *bomb* or *nerve gas*.[23]

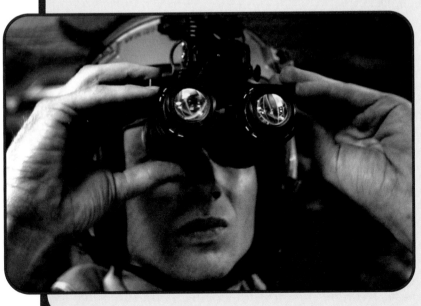

Down the Road

Eventually some agents earn their intelligence officer certification. This means the agents have completed special training in intelligence work. This certification is required for anyone who wants to be considered for promotion. All special agents receive regular advancements in rank, based on how long they have been on the job.

After some experience with a squad, some agents also get assigned to a special response team.

USERT divers collected evidence off the ocean floor after TWA Flight 800 exploded over the Atlantic in 1996.

This can be very exciting work. The FBI has four Underwater Search and Evidence Response Teams (USERT). These teams of divers are trained to retrieve evidence from underwater. USERT divers collected evidence off the ocean floor after TWA Flight 800 exploded over the Atlantic in 1996. They also worked in Yemen after the U.S. Navy's USS *Cole* was bombed in October 2000.[24]

Every field office has its own evidence response team. These teams are a lot like the ones on the television program *CSI*. The main difference is that CSI

A few agents work on the Underwater Search and
Evidence Response Teams.

teams work for a local police department. The FBI's teams work all over the United States and in other countries. Local, state, and foreign law-enforcement agencies often request their help at major crime scenes.

The San Francisco team went to the scene of the Oklahoma City bombing and the World Trade Center collapse. In 1993, a girl named Polly Hanna Klaas was taken from her Petaluma, California, home and killed.

> The San Francisco team "pored over the crime scene for long hours with specialized equipment." A special agent found a palm print.

The San Francisco team "pored over the crime scene for long hours with specialized equipment."[25] A special agent found a palm print. The palm print tied Klaas's killer, Richard Allen Davis, to the scene of the crime. In 1999, one evidence response team went all the way to the province of Kosovo, in the country of Yugoslavia. They investigated mass graves and other sites of war crimes.[26]

Certain evidence response teams are trained to handle hazardous materials and to rescue hostages. SWAT—special weapons and tactics—teams are called in when special agents need to break into a building.

Thanks to the FBI's Underwater Search and Evidence Response Teams, investigators were able to rebuild part of TWA Flight 800.

In the summer of 1992, a family became involved in a confrontation with the FBI. They lived in Ruby Ridge, Idaho. The father, Randy Weaver, was suspected of being a supporter of the Aryan Nations, a white-supremacist group. Weaver was accused of owning an illegal shotgun. Inside his home, he refused to surrender to law-enforcement officers. His property was placed under surveillance by the U.S. Marshals Service.

One morning Weaver went hunting with his friend Kevin Harris and his teenage son Sam. Suddenly their dog came upon an FBI agent. The agent killed the dog. The boy tried to shoot the agent. The agent then shot him. Sam Weaver died from a bullet in the back. Harris shot and killed another agent.

The next day, the FBI surrounded the Weaver house. When Weaver, his daughter Sara, and Harris left the house, a sniper opened fire. An agent aimed for Harris but instead shot Weaver's wife, Vicki, through the door of their cabin. She was holding their baby when she was shot and killed. For the next ten days, the FBI kept the Weaver house surrounded. Finally Weaver gave himself up.

In court, a jury found Weaver not guilty of all charges except for missing his original court date. Harris also was found not guilty. Many people, including congressmen in a Senate Judiciary Committee hearing, asked questions about the FBI's handling of the Ruby

Ridge situation. They asked whether the FBI tried to hide from the public what happened there. Other people asked why agents shot Sam and Vicki Weaver.

Finally, the FBI undertook its own investigation into the case. Investigators decided that five FBI agents had made mistakes. The FBI agents broke protocol because they shot people when they were not in direct danger. The agency also has promised to be more open with the public about what it does.[27]

FBI agents take a break from collecting evidence at the Pentagon after the September 11 terrorist attacks.

In November 2005, an FBI SWAT team helped raid a Houston house where gang members were known to live.[28] Canine—or K-9—teams use dogs to help find explosives.

Special agents can be promoted to supervisory, management, and executive positions. They might become a special agent in charge—the person in charge of a field office—or an assistant special agent in charge. Higher up, there are section chiefs; assistant directors, who head up the FBI's major divisions; and the director. None of these agents and directors would be able to do their jobs without the help of the FBI support staff.

Several popular television shows have featured FBI profilers. Many people believe the FBI has a huge number of profilers on its staff. This is not true. There are only about forty profilers on the FBI staff. Profilers are special agents who specialize in creating psychological profiles—summaries of people's characteristics that help predict their behavior. Profilers focus on criminals, especially serial killers.

Profiling began in the 1950s. The FBI asked a psychiatrist, Dr. James Brussel, to help catch the Mad Bomber of New York. This criminal had sent a series of bombs to executives and buildings of Con Ed, New York City's electric company. The person also had planted bombs in movie theaters. Dr. Brussel read notes the bomber had sent. He also studied the crime scenes. The doctor used this evidence to guess that the bomber was male and spoke a Slavic language as his first language. Brussel also believed the man was single and lived with his mother or an aunt. Brussel also guessed that the bomber was paranoid. Paranoid people have extreme fears. They often believe they are being treated unfairly, or someone is spying on them.

In time, the bomber provided the final clue to his identity. He told the FBI that he had been injured at a Con Ed plant at a certain time. Agents looked for someone who had been working at Con Ed at that time and who had a Slavic surname. They located George Metesky. This man was convicted of the bombings.

In 1969, a special agent named Howard Teten began to study profiling with Dr. Brussel. A second agent named Pat Mullany joined Teten. Together they formed the Behavior Science Unit. Today the FBI asks special agents with a lot of experience to become profilers. They then get special training.

Profilers look at evidence from the crime scene. They look for clues about a criminal's behavior. Sometimes the way a criminal did something reveals something about his or her personality. Profilers try to decide whether the criminal is "male or female, married or single, employed or unemployed, a local resident or a drifter, organized or disorganized."[29] They try to link similar cases together.

Profiling gets criticized because it is not always reliable and because of concerns about misuse and racial discrimination. But it has had some great successes. For example, Dr. Brussel accurately predicted that the Mad Bomber liked to wear double-breasted suits, buttoned up. The bomber's very neat work and attention to detail made the doctor think he would also wear very neat and conservative clothing. Sure enough, Metesky was wearing a double-breasted suit when he was arrested.

Many people support the FBI agents' work in the field, including forensic examiners. This examiner is reviewing the results of a firearm test.

Chapter 4

Behind the Scenes

Special agents make up almost half of the FBI's workforce. They do most of the work on FBI cases. The public sees special agents more often than other FBI employees. They are the ones who show up in television shows and movies. However, special agents are far from the only people who make the agency successful.

Thousands of people on the FBI's payroll work behind the scenes. Some are managers or administrators. Others are professional people with special skills and expertise. One especially important group is the intelligence specialists. Other professionals at the FBI include forensic examiners, financial analysts, computer specialists, lawyers, and cryptanalysts, otherwise known as code breakers. All of these jobs require a lot of education—at least a college degree. They also require special training, but the hard work pays off in salary and benefits.

The FBI also has a huge support staff of secretaries and computer technicians. The agency hires its own security guards, craftspeople (such as carpenters and

---

The FBI crime lab is huge—it has three towers, each five stories high.

---

plumbers), and maintenance personnel. The people in support jobs need less education and training than professionals. They make less money, too. But every job is important at the FBI.

At the Crime Lab

One especially interesting place to work is at the FBI's new crime lab. For a long time, the crime lab was located in the headquarters building in Washington, D.C. Recently, it moved to its own building in Quantico, Virginia, on the same marine base as the FBI Academy. The crime lab is huge—it has three towers, each five stories high.

Clerical crime-lab employees talk on telephones and update records on computers. They work in regular offices or cubicles. Scientific analysis takes place in labs.

These glass-walled workspaces are filled with special equipment such as test tubes, scales, microscopes, and a machine called the gas chromatograph-mass spectrometer, which is used to analyze chemicals.

The new FBI crime lab cost approximately $155 million to build and is about twice the size of the original lab.

Before entering the sterile lab area, FBI personnel wash their hands and put on lab coats.[1]

The firearms unit can fire weapons in a special room. The arson unit also has its own workspace. Here staff can set fires and put them out. A darkroom is available for photographers to process their photos.

The FBI's crime lab has large storage facilities because it owns many huge collections of items. The collections include different kinds of weapons, bullets, cartridge casings, bomb fuses, timers, poisons, fibers, paint samples, tire treads, and feathers. The list goes on and on.

The FBI crime lab has a staff of approximately seven hundred people. As a group, they are called forensic examiners. The FBI's forensic examiners have backgrounds in many scientific fields. Some are chemists. But there are also biologists, physicists, and toxicologists (experts in poison), as well as other specialists.

Forensic examiners all share certain characteristics. Every one of them is capable of intense concentration. They all know how important it is to prevent evidence from becoming contaminated, or spoiled. As a group, they are extremely careful and organized. They have the patience to keep extremely detailed records. They also need manual dexterity, meaning the ability to use their hands precisely. They have to pick up tiny bits of evidence and place them on microscope slides, for example. Forensic examiners can dress as they please when they are in the office. In the lab, however, they often have to wear lab coats, safety goggles, gloves, and protective hoods.

FBI forensic examiners' jobs, like those of special agents, vary from day to day and case to case. They do

A crime lab employee takes samples of dried blood from a jacket.

different kinds of work based on the evidence at hand and what questions a law enforcement officer has asked them. Some cases come to forensic examiners straight from special agents. Other times forensic examiners help with a case sent from another law-enforcement agency.

Some forensic examiners are biologists. These are the people who do DNA analysis. DNA is the material that carries genetic information inside cells in our

```
DNA carries genetic information
    inside cells in our bodies.
   It can be used to identify
     a criminal or a victim.
```

bodies. DNA is present in most of our cells. It is found in our skin, hair, bones, and saliva. Except for identical twins, who share the same DNA, it is unique in every person. Special agents and other law-enforcement personnel collect material such as a strand of hair or a person's drinking glass. Then DNA analysts try to take out DNA from the items. With the DNA they can often identify either a criminal or a victim.

Forensic anthropologists work with bones. First they look at bones to determine if they come from a human. Then they look at certain bones and teeth to determine the age of a victim. To figure out whether a skeleton belonged to a male or female, they may look at the skull. Men's and women's skulls are slightly different. The hips and pelvis also help determine a person's gender.

Forensic anthropologists also gather clues about a person's life history, including injuries or diseases they have had. Skeletons provide clues about how a person died. Another interesting group of forensic examiners are the forensic sculptors—often anthropologists. They reconstruct faces by adding clay to a skull to reveal what a victim looked like.

Forensic chemists do toxicology work, seeking to identify poisons. They also analyze car paints and explosives. Metallurgists know all about different metals. Documents analysts examine documents to see if they are altered or fake. Computer forensic examiners can get data off computers, even after the user has deleted it.

Uncovering Clues at Columbine

When the Columbine High School shooting took place in 1999, the FBI crime lab led the way in collecting information about the crime scene. Videotapes from the school's cafeteria area were sent to the lab's Forensic Audio, Video, and Image Analysis Unit. There the tapes were duplicated and then enhanced. Their contents became clearer. Analysis by video specialists helped investigators figure out exactly what happened that tragic day. Computer specialists also contributed by restoring data that had been erased from the shooters' computers.

Fingerprint Analysis

Every day, all over the world, police evidence teams collect fingerprints from the scenes of crimes. Prints on shiny objects, such as a drinking glass or a doorknob, can be easy to see. Investigators use special lights, chemicals, and powders to find latent fingerprints. Latent fingerprints are invisible to the naked eye. Sometimes investigators take photographs of prints. Other times they use tape to lift prints from a surface.

Crime-lab technicians have special ways to bring out tricky prints. They might apply superglue to a latent print. This can make it visible. They can even find very old prints. To do this, they use vacuum metal deposition. Using this technique, they put an object, such as a gun, into a pressure chamber. Then they pump all the air out. They fill the chamber with two metals—gold and zinc—in gas form. When the metals cool and condense into a solid, they stick to fingerprints' ridges. This makes the prints visible.

Fingerprints provide clues to suspects. They also help identify victims. When police forces need to identify fingerprints, they turn to the FBI's Integrated Automated Fingerprint Identification Systems (IAFIS). At one time, the FBI collected fingerprints on cards. It was difficult to match prints. Today fingerprints are stored in computer databases. The computerized system analyzes a print. It looks for individual ridge characteristics—points where a ridge ends or is broken up. Then the system goes through its records to find similar prints. It is up to an examiner to confirm a match between the system's records and the actual fingerprint. Today IAFIS stores the prints of millions of people. These include not only criminals but also government employees and other people whose fingerprints have been recorded. The FBI trains other law-enforcement agencies in basic fingerprint analysis and finding latent fingerprints.

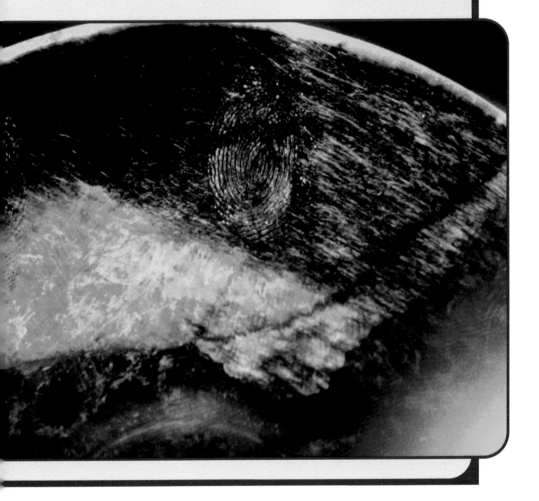

Cryptanalysts decode secret messages written by spies, terrorists, and other criminals. Structural design experts know all about buildings and how they are built. They help special agents understand what happened in a building that has been bombed, for example.

In addition to doing lab work, FBI crime-lab personnel train state and local forensics specialists. They train people on fingerprint identification, DNA analysis, hair and fiber examination, firearms identification, document examination, bomb disposal, polygraph testing, shoe-print and tire-tread analysis, and artist sketching.

The FBI's crime lab does approximately 1 million case examinations each year.[2] Crime-lab personnel are proud of the success in the Lockerbie case. They also did great work after the April 1999 shootings at a high school in Columbine, Colorado. In that case investigators used video recorded by cameras in the school's cafeteria to discover what happened at the school. The FBI lab also helped identify criminals in the Kosovo War in 1999. It played a huge role in learning the identities of the hijackers of September 11, 2001. Entire books have been written about single FBI crime-lab cases.

Forensic examiners make between roughly $50,000 and $100,000 per year, depending on their qualifications and experience.[3] People with advanced degrees and special skills or supervisory jobs make more money than examiners with less education and experience.

FBI Intelligence Analysts

When the FBI made counterterrorism its top priority after September 11, the agency needed many more intelligence analysts.[4] There are three types of intelligence analysts. All-source analysts go through already gathered intelligence. They look for patterns and try to understand what criminals are planning to do next. Operations specialists go out into the field and collect intelligence. Reports officers work to identify important information from FBI investigations and

FBI Jobs at a Glance

Position	Salary
Secretary	$29,000 to start
Evidence technician	$31,000–$55,000
Intelligence analyst	$50,000 to start
Forensic examiner	$50,000–$100,000
Special agent	$43,441 to start
Special agent supervisor	$100,000 to start

intelligence reports. They bring this information together into a complete report to share with appropriate FBI officials, law-enforcement agencies, and other federal agencies like the CIA. Intelligence analysts work in FBI offices all over the United States and around the globe. In 2006, the agency needed analysts to fill vacancies in Amman, Jordan; Berlin, Germany; London, England; Mexico City; Tel Aviv, Israel; and Paris. Intelligence analysts' salaries started at about $50,000 in 2006.[5]

As of 2006, the agency was still working hard to hire more intelligence analysts, but the jobs were

Intelligence analysts work in FBI offices all over the United States and around the globe.

hard to fill. The agency especially needed people with expertise in weapons of mass destruction, counterterrorism, Islamic studies, and international banking. It was looking for people fluent in languages such as Farsi, Urdu, Pashtun, and Dari. It needed people knowledgeable about affairs in Korea and China.[6]

The FBI was having trouble finding qualified applicants, so it began to train some people before they even applied for jobs. According to journalist

Special Agent

The FBI works around the world. An FBI agent (right) trains Hungarian police officers.

Tickahorn Hill, both the FBI and the CIA have started to work with colleges and universities:

> [They] offer scholarships to students who promise to work for them and they create programs and courses— such as introduction to intelligence analysis and research and analysis—to enhance the pool of applicants.[7]

Women at the FBI

In the early twenty-first century, FBI officials expressed frustration at how hard it was to recruit women to join the force. One applicant coordinator said that many women believed they would not be qualified for the job. Some women thought the agency would not want them. They worried about the agency's strict physical requirements.

There are ways women are especially suited to FBI jobs, however. Research shows that women are good at interpreting people's facial expressions. They can quickly change how they relate to the world. This makes it easier for them to adjust to change. Women approach problems differently from men. Often they are better at seeing patterns. Women also can often handle emotionally charged situations better. They can help people feel less stress or tension. So the best FBI teams include both women and men.

The FBI has tried to attract women by letting special agents work part-time. This helps women because so many care for a child or an aging parent.[8]

Women have held many important positions at the FBI. Women have served as both FBI assistant director and head of important field offices, including London and Las Vegas.[9]

There is little specific information about training available to the public. However, the FBI conducts in-house training of intelligence analysts through the College of Analytic Studies. It was established in October 2001 and it is located at the FBI Academy in Quantico, Virginia. The College of Analytic Studies offers the six-week Basic Intelligence Analyst Course, along with other training.[10]

Intelligence analysts' most important job assignments involve preventing terrorism. They also get other types of assignments, however. For example, FBI intelligence analyst Milton Ramirez described bringing down a violent gang in Puerto Rico. His team knew the gang had taken over a housing project. It sold drugs and hid illegal firearms there. The gang was forcing residents of the complex to hide drugs for them. The residents were terrified. They did not go to the police because they feared the gang.

Slowly FBI analysts figured out who belonged to the gang and how it was organized. They figured out how gang members communicated. The gang's lookouts used two-way radios to warn each other of the approach of law-enforcement officers. Agents gathered evidence of the gang members' activities. Their work resulted in many arrests.[11]

Intelligence analysts have also been credited with vital successes outside of the United States. In September 2005, a major weapons dealer was put behind bars thanks to intelligence gathered about shoulder-to-air missile sales from Russia.

Financial Analysts

Financial analysts investigate white-collar crimes, such as health care fraud, against the government. They look for evidence that government money has been stolen or misused. They might search a government official's financial records for evidence that he or she accepted a bribe. At the Terrorist Financing Operations Sector, analysts try to find out where terrorists get their money and what they do with it. One financial analyst, whose full name the FBI will not reveal, analyzes bank accounts. She watches money flow in and out. Sometimes she looks at a suspect's spending to help special agents understand their behavior.[12]

Language Specialists

The FBI needs a vast number of language specialists to act as translators and interpreters. In 2006 the agency had more than a thousand language specialists working at FBI headquarters and in fifty-two field offices. These workers translate documents and speak to criminals and law-enforcement officials in foreign countries. FBI employees speak more than fifty languages. One language specialist is Dr. George Kim. He had a long career as an engineer before he was hired by the FBI because of his fluency in Korean.[13]

Special Agent

The specialist who calls herself Katrina speaks Russian. Katrina has been trying to crack a case of Russians who were smuggling people into the United States. She went to Moscow with the FBI director to act as one of his interpreters. She also traveled to Alaska. There she interviewed Russian crewmembers of ships whose captains were charged with serious environmental crimes.

Support Positions Requiring Special Skills

Many FBI jobs do not require extensive schooling, but they do require a special skill. For example, the agency employs firearms instructors, nurses, locksmiths, photographers, pilots, and truck mechanics. Firearms instructors teach FBI personnel and other law-enforcement officers how to handle pistols and shotguns. They have to be expert shots. They also need to be trained in gun safety and first aid.

Nurses work in special FBI medical clinics. They help people who have been hurt on the job. Nurses also perform fitness-for-duty exams and do some counseling. This job requires a nursing degree.

Locksmiths install and open locks on doors and safes. They also cut keys. Special training is required for this work.

Photographers work with field and satellite offices as well as in the crime lab. They are asked to take many different sorts of photographs. Sometimes they go to crime scenes. Other times they take surveillance photographs. They even take photographs from the sky. The FBI's photographers know how to use many special types of cameras and scanners. They process photos, print them, and send them to archives for safekeeping. Sometimes they produce images to be used in court.

The FBI has its own fleets of airplanes and vehicles. They employ pilots, drivers, and mechanics. Pilots sometimes fly FBI staff from one place to another. Other times the pilots fly special spy planes. Nightstalkers, for example, are equipped with infrared equipment. This lets agents track people and cargo even as they move in the dark. Other planes are used in electronic surveillance. This happens when agents want to follow a suspected terrorist with a bugged cell phone, for example.[14]

Other Support Positions

The FBI also fills many support jobs. These jobs require a clever mind and a responsible attitude, but applicants need no special schooling or skill. Most support jobs require a high-school diploma but no further education.

One type of support job is the evidence technician. Evidence technicians work in field offices. They handle evidence that special agents have collected. They receive evidence, identify and store it, and complete necessary paperwork. They store evidence in an Evidence Control Room or other approved location. Some of the evidence, such as hazardous materials, is dangerous. Evidence technicians need special training in how to handle, store, package, and send these materials. Sometimes they have to testify in court regarding chain of custody, meaning the technicians provide information as to how evidence has been handled. Chain of custody

Evidence technicians need special training in how to handle, store, package, and send hazardous materials.

is important because American law says that law enforcement agents must keep evidence safe and handle it with extreme care. The technicians do not analyze evidence, however.

Electronics technician is another crucial support job. These employees maintain the agency's electronic equipment. The agency also has its own police officers or security personnel. Agency offices also need secretaries, file clerks, and janitors.

Support jobs' salaries vary widely. They pay well compared with other workplaces, however. For example, secretaries at the FBI started out at $29,000 in 2005.[15] Evidence technicians made between $31,000 and $55,000.[16] With good pay and great benefits, a support position may be worth exploring as a career at the FBI.

Members of an FBI SWAT team give a talk about their job to visitors at the Minneapolis FBI office.

Chapter 5

Is the FBI in Your Future?

Recently there has been a lot of change at the FBI. Up until 2001, the agency focused on solving crimes. The FBI still works hard to break up drug rings and hunt down serial killers. However, after September 11, the FBI's focus changed. Today the agency's top goal is to protect the United States from terrorist attacks.

The FBI also has changed the way it is organized. The agency created four new executive positions at the very top of the organization. It also hired more special agents and created many new analyst positions. Today it seeks to hire many more specialists, people with very special skill sets. For example, the agency wants to hire people who speak more languages, especially those spoken in the Middle East and Asia.

The types of people on the FBI's staff have changed the agency, too. Even twenty years ago, there were almost no women or people of color working there. Today the agency tries to hire women and people from diverse backgrounds. Their numbers remain very low, however.

Another change has happened to what cops and other people in law enforcement call information sharing. In the past, the FBI kept a lot of secrets. Today it is much more open and helpful. It provides information and services to state and local law-enforcement agencies.[1] The FBI trains personnel from many other agencies.

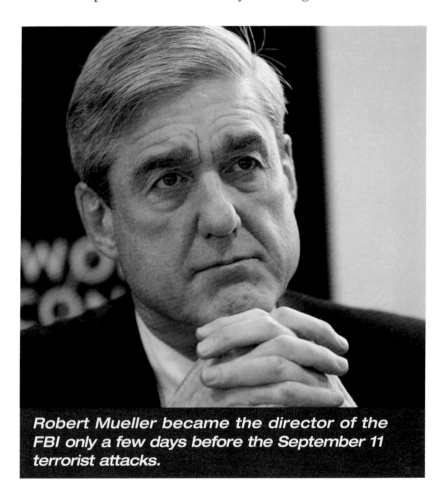

Robert Mueller became the director of the FBI only a few days before the September 11 terrorist attacks.

The FBI On-Screen

The FBI fascinates so many people that it often appears in television shows and movies. At the drive-in movies, your grandparents might have watched *I Was a Zombie for the FBI* or *Invasion of the Body Snatchers*. *The X-Files* was a huge television hit in the 1990s. In that show, special agents Fox Mulder and Dana Scully tried to solve cases involving aliens. Later, viewers tuned in for *Without a Trace* and the Discovery Channel's *FBI Files*. Recent hit movies include Sandra Bullock's *Miss Congeniality* movies and *The Silence of the Lambs*, in which actress Jodie Foster plays a special agent who has to interview a cannibal.

All of these changes have been for the better. Today the FBI director believes the agency has a good reputation and that his agency is much more ready to deal with terrorists than it was in the past.[2] In spring 2006, FBI Director Mueller told Congress,

> This year will mark the five-year anniversary of [the] September 11th [attacks]. The FBI has changed dramatically since the terrorist attacks and we will continue to evolve to meet the emerging threats to our country. We have expanded our mission, radically overhauled our intelligence programs and capabilities, and have undergone tremendous personnel growth.[3]

No one can predict the FBI's future, but some things seem certain. The FBI is in a period of change. The agency can be expected to add more jobs and to change some of its current ones. It will also keep coming up with new crime-solving techniques while adding new technology.

Sometimes the FBI receives help from regular people, such as Tarryn Pitzer, who told authorities about threats made online.

Special Agent

FBI National Academy

The FBI National Academy is a special school for law-enforcement officers. More than fifteen thousand law-enforcement personnel from around the world have graduated from the academy. The National Academy offers courses four times a year in law, behavioral science, forensic science, leadership development, communication, and health/fitness. One of the best things about the National Academy is that officers get to talk about their experiences and create partnerships. Often they work on cases with their fellow classmates after they depart Quantico.

Your Future in the FBI

Has this book interested you in a career at the FBI? Whatever job you consider, you will need to weigh the pros and cons. Working for the FBI has many benefits. The agency's employees feel that their work is important. Special agents and others find their work rewarding. They like that the FBI badge earns them respect.

FBI employees admit that there are drawbacks to working for the agency, too. Special agents and others face danger in their work. Members of the FBI have died in the line of duty. FBI employees find it difficult when their work is criticized. Congressmen, journalists, and members of the public sometimes question the way they handle cases.

The FBI Honors Internship Program

For three months every year, about a hundred students go to work for the FBI. They are interns, part of the FBI Honors Internship Program. Some are students who have just finished their junior year in college. Others are almost finished with graduate school. They have just one more year before they receive a master's degree or a Ph.D. All interns have high grade point averages. When they apply, they must send an essay and a letter of recommendation from their college or university. Before being selected for the program, all applicants have to go through a drug test and a background check.[4]

Interns report to Washington, D.C., where they are assigned to a division. The assistant director of their division supervises them. Interns work with special agents and other FBI employees on important cases. They learn investigative procedures and techniques. A lucky few, who are earning a college degree in the physical sciences, get to work at the crime lab in Quantico.

There are many ways to increase your chances of getting hired by the FBI. Number one is to stay out of trouble. The agency carefully checks all applicants' backgrounds. It looks for past criminal activity, drug use, and even financial trouble. Number two is to stay in shape. Many jobs at the FBI are physically demanding. FBI recruiters also suggest that young people enroll in language classes in high school and college. Applicants who speak a foreign language—or even better, two or more foreign languages—have an advantage.

Recruiters also say it is important to work hard in high school and college. Good grades will help you get a job at the FBI. Some people believe that taking classes or majoring in law enforcement will help them land a job with the agency. In truth, the FBI needs specialists in all kinds of fields. It even has a geologist on its payroll. Remember that the FBI needs accountants and people with law degrees.

Applicants who make it through the hiring process share a couple of attributes. One, they are good at taking tests. The good news is that the skill of test-taking can be improved with practice. Successful applicants also do well in interviews. This skill can be learned through practice, too.

If you think you would like to work for the FBI one day, try to meet with FBI personnel. Some field offices have community outreach programs. The Honolulu, Hawaii, office has an Adopt-a-School Program and a Junior Agent Program. In some cities, agents serve as mentors to inner-city kids.[5]

The one guarantee is that there will always be a need for employees at the FBI. People who choose to join the FBI are certain to find their jobs interesting and important.

Chapter 1. What Happened at Lockerbie?

1. "On This Day: 21 December: 1988: Jumbo jet crashes onto Lockerbie," *BBC News*, n.d., <http://news.bbc.co.uk/onthisday/hi/dates/stories/december/21/newsid_2539000/2539447.stm> (October 31, 2005).

2. "Byte Out of History: Solving a Complex Case of International Terrorism," *FBI Headline Archives*, December 9, 2003, <http://www.fbi.gov/page2/dec03/panam121903.htm> (November 9, 2005).

3. Richard Platt, *Crime Scene: The Ultimate Guide to Forensic Science* (New York: DK Publishing, 2003), p. 117.

4. David Fisher, *Hard Evidence: How Detectives Inside the FBI's Sci-Crime Lab Have Helped Solve America's Toughest Cases* (New York: Simon & Schuster, 1995), p. 69.

5. "Lockerbie Verdict," *PBS Online Newshour*, January 31, 2001, <http://www.pbs.org/newshour/bb/transportation/jan-june01/lockerbie_1-31a.html> (November 9, 2005).

6. "Preparing for the Unthinkable: FBI Participates in Nation's Largest Ever Mock Terrorism Event," *FBI Headline Archives*, April 22, 2005, <http://www.fbi.gov/page2/april05/topoff042205.htm> (April 27, 2005). Wayne Parry, "Officials to Review Anti-Terror Drills," *ABC News*, April 7, 2005, <http://abcnews.go.com/US/wireStory?id=648747&CMP=OTC-RSSFeeds0312> (November 13, 2005). "TOPOFF3 Frequently Asked Questions," *Department of Homeland Security*, n.d., <http://www.dhs.gov/dhspublic/interapp/editorial/editorial_0603.xml> (November 13, 2005).

7. "Facts on the Program," *The FBI's Ten Most Wanted Fugitives*, n.d., <http://www.fbi.gov/wanted/topten/tenfaq.htm> (August 14, 2006).

8. "About Us—Quick Facts," *FBI*, n.d., <http://www.fbi.gov/quickfacts.htm> (August 14, 2006).

9. "Protecting America from Afar—A Few Words with Tom Fuentes of FBI International Operations," *FBI Headline Archives*, September 12, 2005, <http://www.fbi.gov/page2/sept05/protectingamerica091205.htm> (November 13, 2005).

10. "Understanding Contemporary Law Enforcement Intelligence: Concept and Definition," *U.S. Department of Justice*, n.d., <http://www.cops.usdoj.gov/mime/open.pdf?Item=1393> (November 4, 2005).

Chapter 2. A Short History of the FBI

1. "Timeline of FBI History," *FBI*, n.d., <http://www.fbi.gov/libref/historic/history/historicdates.htm> (September 27, 2005).

2. James G. Findlay, "Memorandum for the Director, November 19, 1943," *FBI History—Documents from the Bureau's Founding*, n.d., <http://www.fbi.gov/libref/historic/history/historic_doc/findlay.htm> (November 9, 2005).

3. "Alphonse Capone, aka Al, Scarface," *Federal Bureau of Investigation Famous Cases*, n.d., <http://www.fbi.gov/libref/historic/famcases/capone/capone.htm> (April 27, 2006).

4. "German Espionage and Sabotage Against the U.S. in World War II," *U.S. Navy*, n.d., <http://www.history.navy.mil/faqs/faq114-2.htm> (September 29, 2005).

5. Henry Schuster, "The Al Qaeda Hunter," *CNN.com*, March 2, 2005, <http://www.cnn.com/2005/US/03/02/schuster.column/index.html> (September 29, 2005).

Chapter 3. Agents at Work

1. "Little Progress in FBI Probe of Anthrax Attacks," *Washington Post*, September 16, 2005, <http://www.washingtonpost.com/wp-dyn/content/article/2005/09/15/AR2005091502456_pf.html> (November 13, 2005).

2. Jerry Mitchell, "Senator eyes cold-case unit for civil rights killings," *The Clarion-Ledger*, June 12, 2005, <http://www.clarionledger.com/apps/pbcs.dll/article?AID=/20050612/NEWS010702/506120340/1240> (November 13, 2005).

3. Ryan Turner and Rachel Kosa, "Cold Case Squads," *Bureau of Justice Assistance Bulletin*, n.d., <http://www.ncjrs.org/html/bja/coldcasesquads/index.html> (November 13, 2005).

4. U.S. Department of Labor, Bureau of Labor Statistics, "Police and Detectives," *Occupational Outlook Handbook*, modified May 18, 2004, <http://www.bls.gov/oco/ocos160.htm> (September 30, 2005).

5. "California Terror Plots Foiled: Intelligence Sharing was Key," *FBI Headline Archives*, September 1, 2005, <http://www.fbi.gov/page2/sept05/ca_indict090105.htm>

(October 31, 2005). Barry Newhouse, "4 Men Indicted in California Terror Plot," *Voice of America News*, September 1, 2005, <http://www.voanews.com/english/archive/2005-09/2005-09-01-voa7.cfm?CFID=109772&CFTOKEN=15141553> (November 13, 2005).

6. "Three arrested in missile-smuggling cases," *CNN.com*, August 13, 2003, <http://www.cnn.com/2003/US/08/12/terror.arrest/index.html> (August 14, 2006).

7. "An FBI Insider and Admitted Spy," *CNN.com*, n.d., <http://www.cnn.com/SPECIALS/2001/hanssen/> (November 13, 2005). "FBI History—Famous Cases—Robert Philip Hanssen Espionage Case," *FBI*, n.d., <http://www.fbi.gov/libref/historic/famcases/hanssen/hanssen.htm>. "FBI History—Famous Cases—Aldrich Hazen Ames," *FBI*, n.d., <http://www.fbi.gov/libref/historic/famcases/ames/ames.htm> (November 13, 2005). "FBI Director's Statement on Arrest of Robert Hanssen," *The Centre for Counterintelligence and Security Studies*, February 20, 2001, <http://www.cicentre.com/Documents/DOC_Hanssen_FBI_Director_Statement.htm> (November 13, 2005).

8. "The Case of the Hacked South Pole," *FBI Headline Archives*, July 18, 2003, <http://www.fbi.gov/page2/july03/071803backsp.htm> (November 13, 2005).

9. "Recovery—Backflap," *FBI Art Theft Program*, n.d., <http://www.fbi.gov/hq/cid/arttheft/southamerica/peru/peruvian.htm> (November 13, 2005).

10. "Cracking Down on Public Corruption—Why We Take It So Seriously . . . and Why It Matters to You," *FBI Headline Archives*, June 20, 2005, <http://www.fbi.gov/page2/june05/obrien062005.htm> (October 31, 2005).

11. "Considered a Career as an FBI Special Agent?" *FBI Headline Archives*, March 11, 2005, <http://www.fbi.gov/page2/march05/upclose031105.htm> (April 27, 2006).

12. "Law Enforcement Jobs with the Federal Government," *Federal Jobs Net*, n.d., <http://federaljobs.net/law.htm> (April 27, 2006).

13. "FBI Recognized as Top Government Employers By Readers of Careers and Disabled," *States News Service*, March 23, 2006, <http://www.lib.utexas.edu/ezauth.php?url=http://web.lexis-nexis.com/universe/> (April 27, 2006).

14. "Ask the FBI: Employment Opportunities," *USATODAY.com*, January 21, 2005, <http://www.usatoday.com/community/chat/2001-01-18-fbiemp.htm> (September 30, 2005).

15. "FBI Recruiting Information Technology Personnel," *States News Service*, December 23, 2005, accessed through LexisNexis Academic (April 14, 2006).

16. "The Female Special Agent Web Site," *FBIJobs*, n.d., <https://www.fbijobs.com/fsafaq.asp>. (September 30, 2005).

17. "Phase I Testing," *FBIJobs*, n.d., <https://www.fbijobs.gov/phase1.htm> (November 4, 2005).

18. "FBI—Employment—Special Agents," *FBIJobs*, n.d., <https://www.fbijobs.com/JobDesc.asp?src=001&requisitioni d=368> (September 30, 2005).

19. Julie R. Linkins, "FBI Academy," *FBI Law Enforcement Bulletin*, V. 66, May 1997, accessed through Academic Search Premier, (September 30, 2005).

20. "Firearms Training wins contract with FBI, NYPD," The *Atlanta Business Chronicle*, June 3, 1997, <http://www .bizjournals.com/atlanta/stories/1997/06/02/daily10.html> (April 27, 2006).

21. "Carnivore diagnostic tool, testimony of Donald M. Kerr before Congress," *FBI*, September 6, 2000, <http://www.fbi .gov/congress/congress00/kerr090600.htm> (April 27, 2006). "Big Brother could be reading your e-mails," *The Stanford Daily online edition*, February 21, 2001, <http://daily.stanford .edu/tempo?page=content&id=91&repository=0001_article> (October 4, 2005).

22. "FBI flying planes over U.S. to track suspected terrorists," *FOXNews.com*, March 14, 2003, <http://www.foxnews.com/ story/0,2933,81127,00.html> (April 27, 2006).

23. Ephrain Schwartz, "FBI phone tapping and located cell phones making 911 calls," *Infoworld*, n.d., <http://www.infoworld .com/articles/op/xml/01/01/15/010115opwireless.html> (April 27, 2006).

24. "FBI Dive Teams: Underwater Evidence Collection," *FBI Headline Archives*, August 8, 2005, <http://www.fbi.gov/ page2/aug05/diveteam080805.htm> (October 31, 2005).

25. "Evidence Response Team—San Francisco Unit," *FBI*, n.d., <http://www.fbi.gov/hq/lab/ert/ertsanfran.htm> (November 13, 2005).

26. "Kosovo: Claiming Clues from the Rubble," *FBI*, n.d., <http://www.fbi.gov/hq/lab/ert/kosovo/kosovo.htm> (November 13, 2005).

27. "SWAT Team Members: FBI shooter rules 'crazy' at Ruby Ridge," *CNN.com*, October 14, 1995, <http://www.cnn.com/US/9510/ruby_ridge/> (November 8, 2005).

28. "Federal SWAT team kills 2 men in anti-gang initiative," *Houston Chronicle*, November 5, 2005, <http://www.chron.com/cs/CDA/ssistory.mpl/metropolitan/3440321> (November 13, 2005).

29. Sally Kalson, "FBI profilers help police narrow list of suspects down to one," *Pittsburgh Post-Gazette*, September 28, 2000, <http://www.post-gazette.com/regionstate/20000929profiler3.asp> (November 13, 2005). Brian Innes, *Bodies of Evidence* (New York: Readers Digest Press, 2001), pp. 239–241.

Chapter 4. Behind the Scenes

1. "FBI unveils new crime lab at Quantico," *Free-Lance Star*, April 25, 2003, <http://fredericksburg.com/News/FLS/2003/042003/04252003/955552/index_html> (November 13, 2005).

2. "Laboratory Home Page," *FBI*, n.d., <http://www.fbi.gov/hq/lab/labhome.htm> (April 27, 2006).

3. "FBI Job Announcement Number 18-2006-0024: IT Specialist (Forensic Examiner)," *FBIJobs*, November 10, 2005, <http://www.fbijobs.gov> (November 13, 2005).

4. Dan Eggen and Walter Pincus, "Report: FBI Analyst Jobs Remain Vacant," *Washington Post*, May 5, 2005, <http://www.washingtonpost.com/wp-dyn/content/article/2005/05/04/AR2005050402185.html> (October 29, 2005).

5. "FBI Job announcement FO-2006-0079," *Quickhire*, April 18, 2006, <https://jobs1.quickhire.com/scripts/fbi.ex/runjobinfo> (April 27, 2006). "FBI Job LEGAT-2006-0017," *Quickhire*, April 15, 2006, <https://jobs1.quickhire.com/scripts/fbi.ex/runjobinfo> (April 27, 2006).

6. "FBI job announcement FO-2006-0079," *Quickhire*, April 18, 2006, <https://jobs1.quickhire.com/scripts/fbi.exe/runjobinfo> (April 24, 2006).

7. Tickahorn Hill, "Intelligence analysts in high demand," *Navy Times*, January 30, 2006, <http://www.navytimes.com/story.php?f=1-292313-1475361.php> (April 27, 2006).

8. "Female Special Agent Website," *FBIJobs*, n.d., <http://www.fbijobs.com/fsa/knights.asp> (October 4, 2005).

9. "Leading Ladies of the FBI," *FBIJobs*, n.d., <https://www.fbijobs.com/fsaleading.asp> (October 4, 2005).

10. "Statement of Maureen Baginski," *FBI*, August 4, 2004, <http://www.fbi.gov/congress/congress04/baginski080404.htm> (April 27, 2006).

11. "Considered a Career as an FBI Intelligence Analyst?" *FBI Headline Archives*, January 14, 2005, <http://www.fbi.gov/page2/jan05/intell011405.htm> (April 27, 2006).

12. "Considered a Career as an FBI Financial Analyst?" *FBI Headline Archives*, December 3, 2004, <http://www.fbi.gov/page2/dec04/upclose120304.htm> (October 4, 2005).

13. "Considered a Career as an FBI Language Specialist?" *FBI Headline Archives*, October 10, 2004, <http://www.fbi.gov/page2/oct04/linguist100104.htm> (October 4, 2005).

14. "FBI spy planes patrol US," *Times Herald*, March 15, 2003, <http://www.timesherald.com/site/news.cfm?newsid=7381014&BRD=1672&PAG=461&dept_id=33380&rfi=6> (April 27, 2006).

15. "FBI Job Announcement HQ-2006-0003," *FBIJobs*, November 8, 2005, <http://www.fbijobs.gov> (November 13, 2005).

16. "FBI Job Announcement EP-2006-0013," *FBIJobs*, n.d., <http://www.fbijobs.gov> (April 24, 2006).

Chapter 5. Is the FBI in Your Future?

1. Robert S. Mueller, III, "FBI Reorganization," *FBI*, May 8, 2002, <http://www.fbi.gov/congress/congress02/mueller050802.htm> (October 27, 2005).

2. "Department of Justice FBI's Report to the National Commission on Terrorist Attacks Upon the United States," *FBI*, n.d., <http://www.fbi.gov/publications/commission/9-11commissionrep.pdf> (October 1, 2005).

3. Robert S. Mueller, "FBI Oversight: testimony before the U.S. Senate Committee on the Judiciary," *Federation of American Scientists,* May 2, 2006, <http://www.fas.org/irp/congress/2006_hr/050206mueller.html> (August 14, 2006).

4. "FBI Jackson Applicant/Recruiting Program," *Jackson FBI,* n.d., <http://jackson.fbi.gov/applican.htm> (April 27, 2006).

5. "Honolulu Outreach," *Honolulu FBI,* n.d., <http://honolulu.fbi.gov/outreach.htm> (April 27, 2006). "Weed and Seed," *U.S. Department of Justice,* n.d., <http://www.usdoj.gov/usao/ct/weedseed.html> (April 27, 2006).

anthropologists—Scientists who study the development of humans.

attaché—The person assigned to an overseas mission; a diplomat.

blackmail—The act of getting something from someone by threatening him or her.

bootleggers—People who make alcohol illegally.

carbines—Short-barreled rifles.

condense—To change from a liquid to a solid form.

contaminated—Spoiled by something from the outside; dirtied.

convicted—To be found guilty of a crime.

corruption—Doing wrong by unlawful means, such as bribery.

crime lab—A laboratory where scientists analyze evidence in order to solve crime.

cyber crime—Crime committed using a computer.

dilettante—A person who has limited knowledge of many subjects.

espionage—Spying.

extremists—People with very strong beliefs who carry those beliefs out in extreme ways, sometimes through violence.

federal—Having to do with the national government as opposed to the state or local government.

forensic scientists—Specialists who study evidence found at a crime scene.

fraud—Trickery; lying.

fugitives—People running from law enforcement.

hackers—People who use computers illegally to get information from other people's files.

hostage—A person who has been kidnapped and whose freedom is offered in exchange for something the criminal wants, such as money.

infamous—Well known for doing something evil or dangerous.

intelligence—Information secretly collected by law enforcement personnel.

investigation—A careful search for information about a crime, event, or person.

law enforcement—People and organizations that make sure people obey laws.

paranoid—Extremely fearful and suspicious.

pirated—Illegally copied.

polygraph—A machine that measures physiological processes like heartbeat and blood pressure, used to detect lying.

probationary period—An amount of time after a person is hired when he or she is being watched carefully to make sure he or she is doing a good job.

prohibited—Disallowed; prevented.

qualifications—Skills or experiences that make a person good for a certain job.

radical—Extreme; tending to depart from what is normal or acceptable.

reformers—People who want to make certain changes to society.

rival—Competing; relating to an enemy.

sabotage—The deliberate destruction of something in order to hinder a particular group or country.

saboteurs—People who destroy something in order to hinder a particular group or country.

sanctions—Punishments.

smugglers—People who transport goods illegally.

sterile—Free of germs and living organisms

sting operation—A procedure designed to catch a person committing a crime. It usually involves law-enforcement officials working undercover.

subversives—People who want to overthrow a government.

surveillance—The act of watching a person, group, or place, usually secretly.

suspects—People who might have committed (or helped commit) a crime.

terrorism—The unlawful use of violence in order to try to destroy a government or change a society.

toxicologists—Scientists who study poisons.

traitor—A person who becomes disloyal to his or her country or group.

white-collar crime—Nonviolent crime committed by businesspeople or other professionals, such as tax fraud or money laundering.

Books

Fine, Jil. *Undercover Agents*. New York: Children's Press, 2003.

Keeley, Jennifer. *Deterring and Investigating Attack: The Role of the FBI and CIA*. San Diego: Lucent Books, 2004.

Levitas, Michael, ed. *A Nation Challenged: A Visual History of 9/11 and Its Aftermath* (Young Reader's Edition). New York: New York Times and Scholastic Nonfiction, 2002.

Platt, Richard. *Crime Scene: The Ultimate Guide to Forensic Science*. New York: DK Publishing, 2003.

Ramaprian, Sheela. *The FBI*. New York: Children's Press, 2003.

Internet Addresses

The FBI's home page
<http://www.fbi.gov>

FBI for the Family
<http://www.fbi.gov/fbikids.htm>

U.S. Department of Justice
<http://www.usdoj.gov>

mechanic, 99–100
metallurgist, 89
Most Wanted Terrorists List,
  36
Mueller, Robert, 38–39, 105

N

Nixon, Richard M., 34
nurse, 99

P

Pan Am Flight 103, 7–11
photographer, 86, 99–100
pilot, 99–100
professional positions, 83
profiler, 80–81

R

Red Scare, 32
Roosevelt, Franklin D., 32
Roosevelt, Theodore, 24
Rosenberg, Ethel and Julius,
  32
Ruby Ridge, Idaho, 76–77
Russia, 24, 32, 34, 98, 99

S

secretary, 21, 84, 93, 101
security personnel, 101
September 11, 2001 attacks,
  16, 20, 36, 38, 39, 70, 92,
  93, 103, 105

Soviet Union, 32, 33, 34, 50
special agent, career details,
  43, 44–45, 46–48, 50, 52,
  54–64, 65, 66–67, 68–69,
  70, 71, 72, 74, 79
structural design expert, 92
student programs, 97, 108
support personnel, 20–21,
  83–84, 99–101
surveillance, 33, 46, 65, 71,
  76, 100
SWAT teams, 69, 74, 79
system engineer, 59

T

Ten Most Wanted Fugitives
  list, 18
terrorism, 14, 20, 35–37,
  47–48, 50, 64, 97

U

Unabomber, 44

W

Watergate, 34
weapons, 65, 66, 68–69
women, recruitment of, 97

5/10/07